CRITICAL ISSUES IN AMERICAN PUBLIC EDUCATION

Horace Mann Lecture
1964

CRITICAL ISSUES IN AMERICAN PUBLIC EDUCATION

BY

JOHN K. NORTON
Professor Emeritus, Teachers College
Columbia University

2/26/68 pl 1·50

HORACE MANN LECTURES

THE DISCIPLINE OF EDUCATION
AND AMERICA'S FUTURE
By Lawrence D. Haskew, 1959
$1.50

PSYCHOLOGY OF THE CHILD
IN THE MIDDLE CLASS
By Allison Davis, 1960
$1.85

PERSONNEL POLICIES
FOR PUBLIC EDUCATION
By Francis Keppel, 1961
$1.50

EDUCATION AND THE
FOUNDATIONS OF HUMAN FREEDOM
By George S. Counts, 1962
$2.50

A DESIGN FOR
TEACHER EDUCATION
By Paul H. Masoner, 1963
$2.00

THE HORACE MANN
LECTURESHIP

To commemorate the life of Horace Mann, 1796-1859, and in recognition of his matchless services to the American Public School System, the School of Education of the University of Pittsburgh, in cooperation with the Tri-State Area School Study Council, established the Horace Mann Lectureship. The striking and varied contributions of Horace Mann must ever be kept alive and be reemphasized in each generation. It is difficult, indeed, to assess the magnitude of Mann's educational services. Turning from the profession of law, he devoted his life to the study and improvement of education. He, more than any other, can truly be called "Father of the American Public School System." His boundless energy, coupled with a brilliant and penetrating mind, focused the attention of the citizens of his era on the need for the im-

PROVEMENT AND SUPPORT OF PUBLIC SCHOOLS. HIS
SERVICES WERE MANIFOLD. IT SHALL BE THE PUR-
POSE OF THESE LECTURES TO REAFFIRM HIS FAITH
IN FREE SCHOOLS AND TO CALL TO THEIR SERVICE
ALL CITIZENS OF THIS GENERATION. IT IS VITAL
THAT ALL UNDERSTAND THE PURPOSE AND FUNCTION
OF A FREE PUBLIC SCHOOL SYSTEM IN AMERICAN
DEMOCRACY.

THE HORACE MANN LECTURES ARE PUBLISHED
ANNUALLY BY THE UNIVERSITY OF PITTSBURGH
PRESS.

CRITICAL ISSUES

What Shall Be the Place of Public Education in Our Scale of Values?

Men of insight and vision now recognize that education properly conceived and adequately supported is a major and perhaps even supreme constructive force in the healthy growth of individuals and whole societies. Such being the case, it is imperative that we continually examine and reappraise this great social undertaking. This may be done from many approaches and differing viewpoints. This paper seeks to identify and to comment briefly on several critical issues affecting public education in the United States.

3

The first of these is concerned with the importance and value of public education in the public conscience. The future of American public education will be determined more by how our people deal with this question than with any other which affects the viability of public education in our nation.

In our dynamic society a wide range of interests and undertakings vie for the time, energy, thought, and support of the people. These commodities, however, are finite. Choices must be made. My thesis is that one of the choices which we should make is to place education near the top or even at the very top in our scale of priorities. What are the bases for this position?

First, because it has been a major factor in fulfilling the American dream, education should receive top priority in our nation. That dream envisioned a political system founded upon the consent of the governed. The people as a whole were to determine their political destiny. When this goal was envisioned by the American colonists toward the end of the eighteenth century, it was ridiculed by the Western world and marked for destruction by the misnamed Holy Alliance. This part of the American dream has been achieved. We have gradually extended the ballot, and are still in the process of doing so, to include those previously not franchised as well as those partially disenfranchised by disproportionate representation. We accept the mandate of the ballot rather than that of the bullet.

Ours is a stable government. The palace revolution and the military coup are unthinkable in the United States even though we may be entertained by such performances in the imaginative productions of the motion picture industry. To be sure, little groups of extremists of the left and the right arise and exalt their leaders for a time, but they do not triumph. The communists made their bid for power in the United States under cover of the problems and dislocations of the depression of the 1930's. But this attack upon the foundations of government by consent of the governed got nowhere. I cannot recall the name of a single person who, having given

5

his allegiance to communism, had become a serious threat in the political or any other sector of the United States.

Compare this situation with that in a number of the free societies in Europe. France is so divided in its goals that it has to resort to the charismatic influence of an aging military hero to bring a degree of order into its affairs. Even so, an alarming percentage of its citizens vote the Communist ticket. Italy has a Communist Party which attracts one-fourth of its people. Representatives of this party in Italy and in several other countries recently rushed to Moscow to get the word from a new clique which had come into power without the slightest knowledge and consent of the people.

Leaders on the far right who have gained some prominence are easier to recall than those on the far left. The Huey Longs, the Gerald L. K. Smiths, the Joseph McCarthys have gained brief attention and gone their way. More recently a sincere but supremely negative and angry man, hailed by the Ku Kluxers, the Birchers, and other merchants of

6

fear, hate, and prejudice (and generously financed by a few millionaires) has been repudiated by the great majority of the American people.

The significant fact is not that our democracy is constantly under attack by those who would have a take-over by one extreme minority or another. Rather, the great achievement is that the American people, in spite of the problems and pressures of the technological revolution of this century and the peculiar difficulties presented by a racially heterogeneous population, have kept their poise, their judgment, and their allegiance to free institutions and democratic ideals. The continuing efforts to lead us down one road or another toward despotism have been soundly rebuked.

The system of free public education in the United States has had a part in developing our intelligent electorate. And it is not without significance that the part of the country which has most neglected education is most receptive to the mongers of hate and prejudice.

Ours is an open society—one of free communication. Freedom of the press is maintained even to the extent, in some instances, where freedom merges into license and threatens the rights of individual privacy and fair administration of justice.

The American dream had more than the goals of political democracy and free communication. Our forefathers proclaimed that all men are created equal. The curse of class and caste in Europe and indeed in the whole world was to be replaced by a society in which every person was to enjoy the blessings of individual dignity and of equality of opportunity. The heterogeneity of our population in national and cultural background, in religion, and especially in race has constantly threatened progress toward this ideal. But the goal is still there, and substantial advances toward its fulfillment have been and are being made. One of the most influential instruments in the battle to blunt the antagonisms of class and the prejudices of race has been the public school.

One of the stubborn obstacles which stands in the way of progress in the less developed nations is an ingrown opposition to change. Their inability to comprehend and to recognize the significance of new knowledge and to adapt it to pressing needs often outranks poverty as a block to progress. No such block stands in the path of progress in the United States. The people of the United States display the ability to adapt to changing conditions, which is the price of progress if not of survival in the world of today. The transition in thought and action of the American people in the field of foreign affairs between 1920, when isolationism was espoused, and in 1945, when the United States became a major architect of the United Nations, illustrates the point. Another example is the recognition that changed industrial and employment conditions have an impact on the individual which he often cannot deal with solely with his own resources. Unemployment insurance, social security, and other social innovations are the evidence of this recognition.

One by-product of a democratic and stable government, of an open society, of free communication, of a relatively classless society, and of an adaptable people is a superbly productive economy. I would neither over-rate nor underrate this latter accomplishment. Affluence guarantees neither wisdom nor virtue. But given a choice between the temptations of affluence and the degradation of poverty, I choose the former without hesitation. This would be the clear choice of any observant person who has witnessed the curse of poverty as it afflicts more than half of the people of the world. Affluence is offering us the opportunity to banish poverty among the small percentage of our own people oppressed by it. Furthermore, affluence offers an opportunity to help the poverty-stricken nations of the world to rise out of their suffering. To have achieved an economic status which makes the banishment of poverty at home and its alleviation abroad a feasible goal is a unique and epochal accomplishment. The will to use our affluence for these purposes is an even greater achievement.

Separation of church and state and religious freedom were imbedded in our Con-

stitution by the Founding Fathers. The First
Amendment declared:

Congress shall make no laws respecting an establishment of religion or prohibiting the free exercise thereof. . . .

These were among the most radical ideas of
the new Republic. Europe had long suffered
the penalties of mixing politics and religion
and of religious persecution and intolerance.
These sources of conflict and threats to freedom had been transferred to the colonies.
They were strongly entrenched and there was
powerful opposition to the inclusion in the
Constitution of the words quoted above.

The eventual adoption of this amendment
and its further development in the several
states constitute one of the most fundamental
contributions of our nation to the freedom of
mankind. How advanced was this action is
confirmed by the fact that even in 1964 the
Third Ecumenical Conference failed to take,
or at least postponed, decisive action on the
principle of freedom of conscience in religion.

No agency has done more to consolidate
American belief in the principles of separa-

tion of church and state and of religious freedom than has the organization of public education under the control of all the people, as
opposed to plural control by religious factions.
Today the most serious effort to nullify these
great principles circulate around the questions of public support of parochial schools
and the inclusion of religious indoctrination
in the public school curriculum.

We have heard much in recent months
about crime and moral deterioration in the
United States. I would neither depreciate the
threats to our well-being nor panic because
we have to deal with these problems. The
fact is that mounting crime is a postwar phe-
nomenon occurring in many parts of the
world. But against the evidence of moral de-
cline in the United States, I would weigh
the significance of our restraint in the posses-
sion of paramount power. At the close of
World War II we had an opportunity which
would have tempted some nations. I need
not develop the historical fact that at various
times different societies both in the West and
in the East have sought world hegemony. We

had our opportunity in 1945. We had a supremely productive economy, a tremendous
military force, and a monopoly of the bomb.
We could have sought to dominate the world.
The idea to do so never seriously occurred
to us. Rather, we brought our boys home
from Europe too quickly. Then, we played
a major role through the Marshall Plan in
putting Europe on its feet. With this accom-
plished, we offered aid to the less fortunate
parts of the world. Instead of enslaving Japan,
for example, we aided it in all sectors of its
life to move toward freedom and prosperity.
The action of the United States in the years
following 1945 when it possessed paramount
power is a moral performance unmatched in
the history of the world.

From the foregoing we draw two major
conclusions. Our failures are matched by
some superb achievements, and without the
system of free public education developed in
the United States it would have been impossible to have won these victories. Thus,
education deserves to stand high on our scale
of values because of its performance in shap-

ing our free, productive, and compassionate society. Also, education deserves to stand high among our priorities because of the growing recognition throughout the world that it is an indispensable ingredient of social viability. The evidence on this point is both positive and negative.

One can approximately estimate the socio-economic status of a nation by ascertaining the percentage of its literate population. To be sure, literacy is only a first step towards freedom and the abolition of poverty, but it is an essential step. Literacy opens men's minds to new methods, new techniques, and new aspirations. It arouses desire for progress and displaces a stolid and fatalistic acceptance of misery and degradation.

One sees this process operating in the less developed new nations. As leaders gain access to education they are developing in their peoples what has been called the "revolution of expectation." The old superstitions and fatalism are displaced by knowledge and hope.

Acceptance of changed ways of thought and action is the price of modernity. Education is a major means whereby new ways come into acceptance. The new nations generally recognize this fact and are straining their meager resources to provide universal educational opportunity for their people. Education is the best cure for ignorance, superstition, and poverty.

This fact has prompted some scholars to examine the means whereby Western societies have achieved their relatively high degree of freedom and opulence. Studies indicate that one of the major factors in the progress of the West was the early installation of universal education. Certainly the development of education must accompany economic growth. In some Western nations, however, it appears that education was a precursor of economic advance. This also appears to be the case in Japan—the one nation in Asia which has lifted itself out of chronic poverty. Japan set about providing universal schooling several decades before the turn of the century. Early in this century it achieved virtually universal literacy. A recent Japanese study points out that educational opportunity

15

preceded the rise toward modernity and has been a vital factor in Japanese postwar recovery.

The rapid recovery from the ravages of World War II in Europe and in Japan would have been impossible if human resources had not been built up before the war. In countries with developed human resources, our aid had significant effect. In countries without these resources, our aid has been far less effective.

One might wish that historians would give more attention to the role of education in cultural progress and less to meticulous explorations of the genealogies and foibles of kings, emperors, and their consorts and hangers-on. Historical research concerning the influence of education in the upward struggle of mankind, both when education is used effectively and when it is lacking, would add much to our insight. It also might relieve some of the strain of the fruitless memorization which the history student now undergoes.

One of the most insightful comments of the recent political imbroglio came from President Johnson. He pointed out that education, even with a high flavor of propaganda, had its effects and was a foundation upon which freedom could be built. He then commented that this is being demonstrated in Russia where forces which point toward freedom are arising despite the despotic regime.

I will return to the role of education in social and economic progress. Suffice it to say at this point that there is a growing amount of evidence which indicates that without education a nation can go nowhere, but with education it can go anywhere—perhaps even to the moon. This is proved by the experience of nations which lack education and those which have fostered it.

The American people need to understand this great truth far more clearly than they do today. They should understand it to the point that they will place education near the top, if not at the very top, of their priorities. This is not being done today in the United States. Until it is done we will continue to fall short of realizing the full returns which first-rate education for all might yield.

One may summarize my thesis thus far as follows: Ignorance is the great enemy of mankind. It has been throughout the ages and will continue to be wherever it is permitted to exist. Knowledge is the great emancipator. As it grows and is put to work it elevates mankind. Education begets knowledge and is the means of its dissemination. Accordingly, education deserves a high if not the highest priority on our scale of values.

Later sections of the paper will deal with some of the conditions which must be met if fuller benefits from education are to be realized.

WHO SHALL CONTROL PUBLIC EDUCATION IN THE UNITED STATES?

EDUCATION is power. Totalitarian regimes, as soon as they gain control, expand provisions for education and put all its forms under strict and centralized control. Mussolini, after the march on Rome, worked to control education. Hitler followed his example. Communists fully understand the power of education in shaping thought and action and in laying the groundwork for their goal of world dominion. The USSR could not have achieved its present power status without the dynamic development of education. Red China also recognizes the power of education in shaping the goals and advancing the capability of its people. It is making use of education to the limit of its resources.

That free societies also recognize the power of education is shown by the strong attempts of various groups and interests who would control education in Europe and the United States. The major issue in the United States of public policy and the control of education is whether education shall be under the control of all the people through Boards of Education and Boards of Regents, or whether control shall be parcelled out to various groups and special interests.

A thesis of this paper is that control of education by all the people in the United States is essential if it is to serve and enlighten them to the degree and in a manner essential for the maintenance of a free society. By such control, education can be an instrument of accommodation and reconciliation. It can continue to foster that degree of tolerance, if not of mutual understanding and trust, which is the foundation of a society which seeks to be free, orderly, and viable. On the other hand, to the extent that we structure education around our differences, it becomes an agent of the various segments that exercise control over it, and thus can lead toward mistrust, misunderstanding, and divisiveness.

I am not saying that education in a free society should be monolithic. It is consistent with the values of our society that parents may send their children to any type of school which meets certain minimum standards. But exercising this choice must be done at their own expense, in order that the control and financing of public education will not be dispersed.

Let us now proceed to an analysis of some of the interests in the United States which challenge the American principle of keeping public, tax-supported education under the control of all the people.

There are those who would distribute the control of education among religious denominations, of which there are several hundred in the United States, and ten or more sufficient in number to form bases for denominational school systems. It is possible, if not probable, that the adherents of some denominations would wish to keep public schools under secular, unified control. The situation which is developing in Canada is pertinent. Tax revenue in most of Canada is distributed to religious-oriented boards according to the religion of the taxpayer—Protestant and Catholic, with the Jewish community being given little consideration. This has been hailed as a model for the United States. But recent events reveal a strong secession movement which would divide Canada along religious lines. More than religion is involved, to be sure, but the organization of education

21

in Canada has been more on the side of division than of unity.

In the United States, as in other countries, the Roman Catholic hierarchy demands public financing of its parochial schools. The hierarchy in this country has undoubtedly influenced a considerable percentage, if not a majority, of Catholic laymen to support the extension of parochial schools with public financing.

If this should come about, chances are that the divisive factors threatening the degree of unity essential to an orderly society would be enlarged. The result would undoubtedly extend to educational segregation for non-Catholics. Some other religious denominations would feel that their parochial schools should have access to the public purse. Thus, to the differences in race and national and cultural background with which we now contend would be added the old and tragic one of religion. The powerful influence of the public school in reconciling our differences and in creating the degree of understanding essential for the maintenance of a cooperative rather than a contentious society would be severely weakened if not wholly lost.

The purposes, the spirit, and the effect of education in the United States would be profoundly changed if its control were to be distributed among several religious denominations. With few exceptions, education under religious control is focused primarily upon propagation of the particular theological concepts of the denomination involved. This is illustrated by a statement in the Vatican pavilion at the New York World's Fair. It reads as follows:

It is clear that there can be no true education which is not wholly directed to man's last end, and there can be no ideally perfect education which is not Christian education.

Two words in the foregoing quotation are of special significance. The first is "wholly." Education is to be wholly concerned with the theological position of the particular denomination involved. This raises the question as to what consideration would be given to the role of education in a self-governing democracy to equip citizens for individual and pub-

23

lic duties and responsibilities of life here and now.

The other significant word is "Christian." By Christian education, as has been made plain, is meant Roman Catholic education. It alone can be "ideally perfect."

My position is that religion is so personal and sensitive as it concerns the freedom and convictions of the individual, that it should not become the concern of the state, financially or otherwise. We will break down Jefferson's wall of separation between church and state at our peril.

A second major bid for control of education in the United States comes from the labor unions. That organized labor is making an all-out effort to destroy the National Education Association and its affiliated state and local associations is well known by informed persons. This is more than a mere effort to change the pattern of teacher organization in the United States. It is a bid to share control of public education with the legally instituted boards of education. In my judgment, such action would be a fatal mistake. But

24

before justifying this position, let us clear out some of the false isues which confuse this whole question.

Opposition to amalgamation of teacher organization with union labor does not imply opposition to labor unions. They are an essential element in our free American economy. Furthermore, it is recognized that labor unions have played a vital role in the evolution of our free system of schools. Labor has a great stake in maintaining and advancing the strength of public education in the United States.

These considerations, however, do not lead to the conclusion that teacher organizations should become an appendage of union labor. Why not? Background on this question is gained by sketching its history during the past forty or fifty years.

Around 1920, when the movement to democratize and expand the programs of the national and state education associations got underway, the memberships of the National Education Association and of the American Federation of Teachers (allied with the AFL) were both small and approximately equal.

In the decades following 1920 the energy of the AFL, and later of the CIO, was absorbed in the epic battle between labor and management. In the meantime, the NEA and its affiliated state, and local associations built up their membership until they included, in one way or another, close to 100 per cent of public school teachers. The AF of T languished. Until recently it claimed fewer than 50,000 members. Its operations were largely confined to capitalizing on discontent in a few big cities. It was long on agitation, but short on membership. When a professional association took a position on the development of the schools or the status of teachers, the AF of T would take an allegedly "more advanced position," often with little regard for fiscal and other considerations.

In 1956 something happened which alarmed the labor union officers. For the first time, white-collar workers composed of professional, managerial, office, and sales workers outnumbered the craftsmen, industrial, and other blue-collar operatives. In 1919 the number of blue-collar workers in the United States was double that of white-collar workers. The estimate is that by 1970 the number of white-collar jobs will be 25 per cent greater than the number of blue-collar jobs.

This trend is the result of many factors such as automation and the up-grading of the work force in education and technical skill. Each decade brings an increased demand for trained brains supported by complex equipment and a lessened demand for brawn. The same forces which have stricken the coal miners of John L. Lewis and the communities in which they live threaten other major labor groups, including the powerful union of Automobile Workers.

Union leaders, such as Walter P. Reuther, head of the UAW, see the handwriting on the wall. To maintain their membership, power, and income from dues, the AFL-CIO must enroll white-collar workers. But these workers generally have shown little interest in such affiliation. How shall the unions meet this challenge to their power?

One element in their program is a very

27

strong effort to unionize the million and a half public school teachers. If teachers respond to the union call, their example could be capitalized upon to capture other reluctant white-collar groups. In their more relaxed moments, union leaders make it clear that it is the health of the whole union movement rather than that of the teaching profession which is of primary concern in this movement. Otherwise, union labor would leave the teachers to wallow in the snobbery, political obtuseness, and economic inferiority which is the appraisal of their condition by union officials.

It is important to distinguish between labor as a supporter of free public schools and labor as the organizer of teachers. It was recognized early in the rise of the labor union movement that educational opportunity for all was essential if this movement were to prosper. Accordingly, labor has played a major role in establishing the unique system of United States public schools. By so doing, union labor has not only contributed significantly to the evolution of a free society, but has also helped to raise the literacy and political understanding of the rank and file citizen to a level indispensable for effective organization of craft and industrial unions.

There are those who argue that labor's support of public schools calls for affiliation with the AFL-CIO by teachers as an act of simple gratitude. This is a specious argument. The system of public schools in the United States is the product of the leadership of no one group. Many groups and many individual citizens have played vital roles in the evolution of our free schools.

The fundamental issue is the purpose of the schools. Their first mandate is to inform and enlighten all the people, without fear or favor of the special interests of any particular group or class. To an extent found in no other great nation, the public schools of the United States have been the solvent of cleavages and injustices inherent in a society structured along lines of class and caste. The first and inherent purpose of education in a free society is to serve all the people by preparing them for informed and responsible discharge

29

of the duties of individual and social living.

The difficulties of fulfilling this high purpose of public education are always substantial. They would be greatly increased if teachers officially allied themselves with any special interest group. Teachers would be suspected of favoring this group and would inevitably tend to do so. If the teachers of the United States should throw their lot in with the AFL-CIO and become loyal supporters of union labor, their performance in the classroom would be affected. The great majority of citizens and of workers who are not affiliated with labor would suspect the objectivity of the teacher officially allied with one occupational segment. Only about one in five gainfully employed workers are members of the AFL-CIO. Many non-union workers besides the teachers belong to independent professional organizations to which they give their support and loyalty. Would they, with equanimity, send their children to teachers militantly allied with union labor?

Education in a free society must ever strive to be worthy of its name. To the extent that it becomes an agency of group propaganda it compromises its integrity and loses the confidence of the people of a free society.

Some will equate this viewpoint with the denial of full citizenship rights for teachers. Such an equation is not involved. Outside the classroom teachers should fully enjoy the right to participate in the activities of political parties and other organized groups, including membership in the AF of T, if they are so unwise as to do so. The people as a whole also have the right to question the objectivity of a teacher who supports the alliance of education associations with a militant segment of our society.

The right of teachers to organize as they choose is not always honored. This, however, is an expression of the sensitiveness of the public concerning the objectivity of the instruction of their children. Too often it also represents the desire of organized groups with a variety of special interests to force teaching into the particular mold which they espouse.

31

The right to teach with objectivity and with dedication to the development of thinking minds is a precious one for the professional teacher. It is also basic to the preservation and further perfection of a society of free men.

The difficulties of maintaining and furthering the right to teach objectively are numerous. Unfair accusations against teachers, censorship of textbooks, and curriculum distortion by legislative fiat are rife in this period of confusion and militant extremism.

The situation calls for intelligent and vigorous action by those who understand the vital distinction between education and propaganda. Freedom to teach would be more difficult to maintain if teachers, under the pressures of this disturbed period, were to organize as a part of any special interest group.

The strike is a weapon of unior labor even to the point on some occasions of defying the law of the land. Already teachers have done this in a few communities. It is a grave question whether those, who above all others should teach respect for the law, can appropriately defy it.

Although labor objects to a distinction between the attitude of the professional and the laborite, it is a significant distinction. It will be a sorry day if the objectives and methods of teacher organizations become as narrowly crass and economic as those represented by some labor unions. To be sure, the teacher is worthy of his hire, but it would be tragic if the size of his pay check should become the sole or even the principal goal of the teacher and his organization. Teachers, if they are to render their full service to the nation, must always retain an element of dedication beyond the call of routine duty. The independent professional association is most likely to keep a reasonable balance between economic and intangible rewards of teaching.

My position is that teacher organizations should maintain friendly relations with all agencies which seek to maintain and improve our system of free public schools, but should officially ally themselves with no segment of society.

There is a third effort to take over a major area of educational control which deserves special attention. Its potential significance is as yet realized by very few citizens. I refer to the proposal to bring about a major transfer in the control of teacher education. Control of the education of teachers inherently involves a substantial degree of control over all education. The cliché which says that the teacher is the heart of the school contains a large element of truth. And in turn, the preparation of a teacher for his work determines in large degree the kind of "heart" the school will have.

The proposal, reduced to its essence, is that control of teacher education be transferred from the people as a whole through their legally constituted authorities to the colleges and universities of the country. To be sure, the appearance of general public control would be retained in that the states would legally certify teachers, but they would do it in a largely automatic manner on the basis of a baccalaureate degree, the requirements for which would be prescribed by each college or university.

The proposal which would bring this about is stated as follows:

For certification purposes the state should require only (a) that a candidate hold a baccalaureate degree from a legitimate college or university, (b) that he submit evidence of having successfully performed as a student teacher under the direction of college and public school personnel in whom the State Department has confidence, and in a practice-teaching situation of which the State Department approves, and (c) that he hold a specially endorsed teaching certificate from a college or university which, in issuing the official document attests that the institution as a whole considers the person adequately prepared to teach in a designated field and grade level.[1]

The author of this proposal is James B. Conant. Before dealing with his proposed change in the control of public schools, let me emphasize that Conant has made many valuable contributions to the improvement of public education in the past two or three

[1] James Bryant Conant, *The Education of American Teachers* (New York, 1963), p. 210.

decades. From association with him on the Educational Policies Commission and in other connections, I know him as a man of complete integrity and high public purpose. I believe that he has sought to study the complex field of education with objectivity and a sincere desire to improve the public schools. But I also believe that the transfer of the control of teacher education which he proposes would be disastrous in its ultimate effect on the evolution of our free system of public education.

Conant states that his proposal is "a radical suggestion." I doubt that many citizens have thought through the full significance of the transfer of control proposed by Conant. In its essence the proposal would transfer the control of teacher education from what he labels the "educational establishment." He would entrust it to professors of liberal arts colleges and universities, with, of course, the exception of professors of education, whom he includes as part of the establishment.

Let us examine the makeup of what Conant has labeled the "educational establishment."

Mark well what it includes: "organized school administrators, state Department of Education personnel, classroom teachers of various kinds, professors of education, and the executive staffs of such organizations as the School Boards Association and the Parent-Teacher Association (PTA)."[2] Conant states the charge has been made that these groups exercise a control over teacher certification which amounts to "a national conspiracy."[3] He further states: "While I sympathize with the feeling underlying this charge, I cannot agree with the conclusion it expresses."

My thesis is that the differing positions and attitudes of Conant's establishment and those of the typical college professor throughout the past century are the best test of their future influence in shaping public education as it is affected by the control of teacher education. Accordingly, let us look at the record of these two groups in regard to their basic concepts of the purpose and scope of public education.

[2] Conant, pp. 15–16.
[3] Conant, p. 23.

First, let us examine the long and continuing battle concerning the percentage of the population which should be served by public education.

I submit that it is the establishment which has successfully led the people in developing a system of public schools—a system unique in its effort and its success in extending educational opportunity. The battle was fought first at the elementary school level and was won in principle in the nineteenth century. Groups similar to those now composing Conant's establishment bore the brunt of the battle. What part did colleges and universities play? Generally they were uninterested. If they took any position toward universal opportunity at the elementary school level, it was likely to be lukewarm or hostile toward a policy of seeing that every child went through elementary school.

Representatives of the colleges and universities throughout our history have also generally been highly conservative toward the extension of secondary education. It was the Boards of Education who first established

American high schools at public expense. This policy was challenged. It was a Board of Education which fought for the legal right to establish public high schools at public expense. This right was won in the epic Kalamazoo decision of 1872.

It was the establishment which, during the succeeding fifty years, led the battle to ensure that the high school serve all the people. College professors not unanimously, but generally, have stood and still stand for the selective principle. What would happen to the remainder of youths of high school-age has generally been of little concern to the professors.

Few have condemned more severely than Conant the social obtuseness of those who lack understanding of the complexity of a school. He has stated that the professors of the liberal arts and many of their friends often deal with school problems as if the schools "operated in the stratosphere—that is, in a social vacuum." Informed persons know that many professors still so operate.

At the level of higher education one finds

the same opposition to the extension of educational opportunities between the educational establishment and the professors. The slaughter of the innocents which takes place in the first two years of college is something to behold. If this merely involved the elimination of the allegedly unfit and the unwilling it would have substantial justification. Numerous studies have shown, however, that a considerable percentage of those eliminated between the beginning of the freshman year and graduation are good college material so far as basic aptitude is involved. Why does this happen? This brings us to another issue which divides the establishment and the colleges.

The establishment has consistently stood for the principle that a heterogeneous school and college population calls for differentiation of curriculum, according to student aptitude, interest, and goals, in order to make education of value to all. Colleges have generally stood against this principle. Most professors in the liberal arts and sciences have generally been indifferent to the valiant efforts led by the establishment to make the elementary school an institution of success for all in terms of ability rather than the beginning of failure for many. Many professors have been even more restrictive in their attitudes toward the secondary school level of education through the power they exercise over college admission requirements. Conant has referred to this attitude of college professors as follows:

To be sure, it is a convenient fiction to assume all children enter school with the same interests, abilities, preconceived ideas, and return to homes that are culturally identical. It is even more convenient to assume that a community has no interest in a school except as an institution for developing intellectual powers.[4]

Some would open college education only to those who delight in abstractions and verbalisms and revel in the complexities of higher mathematics and foreign language. Others would confine the curriculum at the college level and even lower, if they had their way, to the classics of Ancient Greece and Rome.

[4] Conant, pp. 64–65.

41

It has even been claimed that those who do not delight in such content are uneducable. Some who make this claim offer this content in substantial, well advertised, and expensive volumes in which they sometimes have less than a solely academic interest.

College professors who take the foregoing positions are, to say the least, restrictive in their judgments about possible routes to intellectual development. Those who lead in the United States have achieved their intellectual competence by a variety of routes.

Those who insist that to obtain a college education one must readily conform to a reading grind, in content that is challenging only to the academic mind, have far too narrow a conception of how different individuals achieve intellectual competence.

I charge that the attitude of the typical college professor today toward technical and professional education and other experiences and curriculum which focus on society as it is and the interests of young people as they are is largely responsible for the premature elimination from our colleges of much first-rate college material. This practice is in part responsible for the chronic shortage of enough persons to fill the upper occupational positions our complex society requires.

There needs to be a thorough examination of the so-called standards about which college professors talk so much. The easy thing to do is to eliminate those who do not readily respond to a bookish curriculum limited to what professors like to study, presented in the unchallenging manner characteristic of those whose advancement depends mainly on research and little on first-rate teaching. There is a good deal of truth in the old saw that a professor's idea of heaven is a college without students. The next best thing is a college attended by students who learn in spite of poor teaching, and who docilely respond to a reading grind which too often is distinguished by its amount rather than by the care which goes into its selection.

Most citizens, and perhaps some college professors, do not realize that the United States is unique in its effort to keep its young men and women immersed in theoretical content, and isolated from life as it is, up to age 22. I refer to the fact that nowhere else in the world does one find the counterpart of our four-year colleges of arts and sciences. Elsewhere it is recognized that full-grown men and women cannot wisely be kept in educational monasteries up to ages 21 and 22.

This brings us to a third issue upon which the educational establishment and many college professors differ: the extent to which preparation for teaching should include teaching methods as well as the courses in the subject one is to teach. The favorite straw man of academicians is the claim that the establishment stands for putting major emphasis on how to teach and too little attention to mastery of the subject to be taught. The opposite is the case. It is the academician who insists that each teacher begin anew in the quest for excellent teaching, disregarding all past experience as to how subject matter in the hands of a master of his field can be most effectively communicated to young students.

This accounts for the fact that the most

44

miserable teaching in our educational system often occurs at the college level. This is especially true in the first two years where much college teaching is delegated to younger instructors more concerned with completing requirements for a doctorate or launching into the field of research than with doing a first-rate job of teaching. Their conception of maintaining standards is too often limited to flunking those who do not readily respond to inept and pompous presentation of their subjects. They violate most of the principles which govern good teaching and equate quality instruction with giving low marks and a high percentage of failures.

It is easy to teach those who are both bright and ready conformists. Far more attention at the college level is needed to develop the kind of teaching which retains students who may not be as verbally brilliant and as readily conformist as professors might like, but who could be far more effective members of our society if the content and methods of college instruction were more challenging to them.

45

Probably the most damning appraisal of the situation in many colleges is made by John W. Gardner, President of the Carnegie Foundation for the Advancement of Teaching. He points out that a "crisis in values" has developed in these institutions under which professors exhibit "the crassest opportunism in grantsmanship, job hopping, and wheeling-dealing." He states that to some professors "students are just impediments in the headlong search for more and better grants, fatter fees, higher salaries, higher rank." Gardner takes account of the growing tendency to upgrade research and to downgrade good teaching as a basis for advancement in higher education. A professor is "lured with the promise of minimum teaching duties. . . . Indeed he may be given the promise that he will not have to teach at all." To offset this trend Gardner concludes that university leaders should agree that no new "non-teaching faculty would be hired."

The New York Times editorially puts its finger on the factor which is largely responsible for the conditions which have developed in higher education. It is the shortage of professors which results in a "seller's market" at this educational level. Accordingly, "on too many university campuses the professor who does a competent or even superlative job of teaching can expect relatively little by way of reward. Promotions and increased incomes and status come today from research, publications, and entrepreneurial success in getting grants from the government, foundations, and similar sources." Continuing the editorial, *The New York Times* concludes that steps must be taken to correct the situation. "The prestige of outstanding classroom performance must be elevated by rewarding it both financially and in terms of status." Action is needed to "revitalize a now endangered section of the country's educational system."

How vigorously and rapidly this revitalization will take place, in a situation where professors operate in a "seller's market," in which fabulous sums from government and industry are available for research talent and relatively little for outstanding classroom performance, is open to question.

The basic difficulty in this whole situation is the neglect of adequate support of education at the elementary and secondary school levels. This has resulted not only in poverty among the disadvantaged and slow learners, but has also caused many thousands who have the aptitude for college careers to leave school prematurely. At the same time fabulous sums have been poured into research and development by industry and the federal government. Thus the potential supply of trained talent has been less than possible at the source, while the demand of a technological society has vastly increased. This major mistake in educational policy will be further dealt with in a later section.

The fundamental conclusion at this point is that it would be compounding the felony to transfer control of teacher education from those who compose Conant's establishment, with all of their history and orientation, to college professors with the predilections on public education which many of them have had in the past and, in large degree, hold even today.

Present signs indicate that conditions in the colleges and universities threaten to become worse rather than better in the immediate future. In 1964 enrollment of those seeking college degrees broke all records for the thirteenth consecutive year. Students more than doubled in number in the past decade. The full impact of the postwar increases in births is only just now being felt by the colleges. In the fall of 1964, a record total of 5,320,294 students was registered in all types of colleges and universities, close to an 11 per cent increase over 1963.

In short, the forces which add up to a "seller's market" in higher education and the unfortunate developments inherent in this situation are likely to accelerate rather than diminish, at least in the years just ahead. More than ever the factors which disqualify the collegiate mind for taking over the control of teacher education are in operation.

Had space permitted, this paper might have further contrasted the educational orientation of the establishment and of college and university professors on other issues.

Three have been dealt with, namely, the issues of whether only a small and selected elite shall have full educational opportunity or whether the aim should be to use education as a means of developing all students to the limit of their ability; the issue of whether only a single track curriculum should be offered or whether it should be differentiated to take account of the varied aptitudes and interests of a heterogeneous student population; and the issue of whether mastery of subject matter alone is enough or whether mastery of one's field should be accompanied by preparation for presenting it in a challenging form.

It is the contention of this paper that on all of these issues the educational establishment has a much sounder record than the college academicians. The fact that the American system of education is unique in many respects is the result of a long-time battle by the establishment with little help from, and often the opposition of, the typical college professor.

My position is that to take the control of

teacher education away from the establishment would be disastrous in its effects on the further evolution of the public school as an instrument in the preparation of the American people for their manifold and demanding duties. It is the very people listed in Conant's educational establishment who have contact with the people, the breadth of educational experience, and the will to continue the development of our unique system of public schools.

The people in the State Department of Education, superintendents of schools, classroom teachers, and citizen groups such as local boards of education and members of parent-teacher associations are those best qualified to judge what it takes to staff the classrooms of the complex public school systems of today with their teeming and heterogeneous populations. Nor do I cast the professor of education into the depths of darkness with the eager prejudice shown by most college professors. Professors of education make up the one department in colleges and universities which has consistently sought to see

51

the American school system as a whole with its enormous complexities in pupil personnel and purpose. If their position on education has not been approved by, and has been even beyond the comprehension of many academic professors, perhaps it is the academic professors who need appraisal as well as those who seek to comprehend and to deal with education as the servant of society as a whole.

To turn the vital function of teacher education over to the typical college professor, oriented to a selective conception of education, enamored with a classical and academic content, too often lacking contact with the powerful social forces which beat upon our public schools, and more concerned with research than teaching, would be a shift in control with lamentable effects. Such action would strengthen the forces with autocratic educational conceptions and weaken those with democratic conceptions as to the purposes of this great social enterprise. Transfer of control of teacher education from the educational establishment to the college professors would be a step back toward the class-structured European conception of education, from which Europe now struggles to extricate itself and back toward the idea that educational opportunity, except at the primary level, is a privilege of the few rather than a right and necessity for all.

WHAT SHOULD BE THE SCOPE OF
AMERICAN PUBLIC EDUCATION?

W HO SHOULD ENJOY the benefits of free public education—at what ages and for how long? In this section we are concerned only incidentally with the content of education and training. This very important factor will be dealt with in a later section.

It is proposed that *all* children and youths up to and through age 21 receive the full benefits of free education, appropriate to their condition, individual talents, and to the new and changing demands of our complex society.

Implicit in this proposal is the concept that full educational opportunity for all be a right, not a privilege. The proposal sets no lower age limit for beginning public education for reasons which will be stated shortly. It advocates that education be free through age 21, that is, through the four-year college or other appropriate post-secondary schooling. It proposes that education be free so far as the financial condition of the individual and his parents is concerned—no one should be blocked from full educational opportunity because he or his parents lack funds to pay for it.

This position challenges the theory that public education should be solely or even principally concerned with an intellectual, social, and economic elite. Rather, it affirms that fulfillment of the ideals of equal opportunity and of the intrinsic worth of the individual require that every person receive the benefits of the best possible schooling. This is imperative for the perpetuation and

54

progress of a democratic, technological society.

Earlier in our history we sought to activate this principle by requiring attendance in school of all youths from about age 6 to 16. This provision and its present extensions in age, both higher and lower, meet neither the educational needs of many individuals nor the needs of the kind of society which exists in the United States today.

One of the more radical proposals included in the foregoing positions concerns the age when free public education should begin. It needs to vary according to the environment of the child. In some cases, which fortunately are still exceptional, it should begin within months after the child is born. I refer to situations where birth for profit—increased relief payment—is carried on by the unfortunate and benighted members of our society. The "family" in this situation is often a mother incompetent in most respects and a miscellany of fathers whose whereabouts is unknown at least to the social worker and perhaps even to the mother.

That young children brought up in the environment which accompanies such a situation suffer severe deprivation in most, if not all, phases of their growth cannot be doubted. Benjamin S. Bloom of the University of Chicago recently reviewed hundreds of studies on the shaping of human beings from infancy to adulthood. His findings emphasize the tremendous importance of the first few years of life for all that follows. Change in many characteristics becomes more and more difficult with increasing age. Bloom concludes:

The nature of the individual's pursuit of life, liberty, and happiness may be largely determined by the nature of the environmental conditions under which he has lived in his formative years. Furthermore, although individuals in a democracy may not be equal at birth, much of their inequality at maturity may be ascribed to the lack of *equality of opportunity* if we see opportunity and environmental conditions as partial reflections of each other.[5]

[5] Benjamin S. Bloom, *Stability and Change in Human Characteristics* (New York, 1964), p. 193.

What Should Be the Scope?

The damage done cannot be wholly repaired even when nursery schools are available (and they usually are not) nor by kindergartens, which are available for only about 60 per cent of our children. A child born into and allowed to exist in a sordid environment, who never has a story read to him, who has barely learned to talk by age 6, and who lacks most of the stimuli to learning which an ordinary home provides, begins his school career as a backward child and is likely to continue so until he becomes a dropout at age 16 or thereabout.

This is a problem which must be faced from all angles, although we are concerned here only with schooling. Education begins at birth. If we are going to permit children to be born into a home and community environment which is educationally valueless or even damaging, we must take steps to see that they are at least partly removed from or protected against this environment. This is imperative both as it concerns the rights of the individual and the well-being of society.

To certain people such a proposal will be obnoxious. They will condemn it on several bases. Some will label it communistic and a method of nationalizing children. Slogans will be enough to salve the conscience of such persons. But for those who wish to think and to face the forbidding consequences of social neglect, one example of which is pregnancy for profit (now being carried on into the third generation in increasing numbers), something more effective than sloganizing will be necessary.

Special care of the child at public expense should come into the picture as early as necessary in order that the child not be severely handicapped in his school career and probably throughout life. Arrangements can be such that the child will be entered in a day nursery school at the age which research and experience indicates is essential to the prevention of serious educational liabilities. In such cases, the child would be at home and in contact with his mother and his father, if one is in residence, for a part of each day. In extreme cases, permanent residence in the nursery could be arranged, with full visiting privileges by the parent or parents. Thus, the child would not be separated from his parents, but would be sufficiently separated from an environment which cripples his development at the outset of life.

Nursery school would merge into kindergarten and elementary school. It is recognized that the problem involved in this whole matter is more than an educational one. The factors which add up to cultural degeneration are complex and involve more than the fullest possible use of education. However, educational leadership must carry its full share of responsibility for seeing that deteriorative forces, generated by our complex society on a fraction of our population, are arrested. The added cost involved will be substantial. However, it must be met, as the cost of inaction will be far greater. A later section will deal with the matter of financing this and other added investments in education which must be met.

Let us next consider the role of the kindergarten. The great majority of children should be in the home until age 5. However, this dogmatic statement should not block active experimentation of the value of schooling for children younger than 5. We hear what appear to be extravagant statements concerning the learning ability under proper supervision, of children younger than 5. We should establish the validity or falsity of these claims, taking account of long-run educational gains, if any, and concomitant emotional effects.

In any case, kindergartens should be available for all 5-year-olds. The educational worth of such schooling has been established by over a century of educational experience. Yet no kindergartens are available for about two out of every five children. A major cause of this is a lack of financial support. This and other obstacles to universal educational opportunity beginning at age 5 should be removed.

Let us next examine the situation as it concerns full educational opportunity for those at the upper end of the educational ladder. The 1960 federal census enumerated 4,879,-

825 male persons in the United States aged 17 to 20 inclusive. Of these, 4,298,626 were white and 581,199 were non-white. The numbers and percentages of the foregoing who were neither in school nor working were:

Group		Number	Per cent
White		446,410	10.3
Non-White		118,064	20.3
	Total	564,474	11.6

Thus, more than one-half million male youths aged 17 to 20 were "on the town" in 1960. If all ages 14 to 22 inclusive are included, the number of male youths, who in 1960 were out of school, unemployed, and not in the labor force,[6] rises to 799,432 (636,-561 white and 162,871 non-white).

The conditions in different states vary considerably. The percentages of male youths ages 17 to 20 inclusive who are out of school and unemployed are given below for the United States and for several states.

[6] These are listed in the U. S. Census as not enrolled in school, unemployed, and not in the labor force. The latter phrase means that they have not recently sought work due to discouragement or other factors.

State	Percentages of Males Aged 17 to 20 Out of School and Unemployed, 1960		
	All Males	White	Non-White
U. S.	11.6	10.3	20.3
New York	12.9	11.7	25.5
Pennsylvania	15.4	14.0	32.3
New Jersey	11.2	9.7	23.1
Illinois	10.3	8.9	24.0
California	9.2	8.5	18.0
Mississippi	9.5	8.3	11.2

The effects of migration from the South to northern and western industrial states are strikingly evident in the foregoing figures. New York has a considerably higher percentage of white and non-white 17- to 20-year-olds out of both school and work than does Mississippi. This does not mean that the schools are poor in New York and good in Mississippi; nor does it indicate a depressed economy in New York and a prosperous one in Mississippi. Rather, it is the result of population migration. As agriculture and other industries have been automated in the South, a flood of unemployed, uneducated persons has gone to the North, adding to the slum population, the results of which are well known. This is one of many examples which illustrate that we are a nation, not a series of states with high unscalable walls. Certainly, education in the United States cannot yield maximum dividends if left solely to the vagaries of state and local conditions and initiative.

Present signs indicate that the problem of youth, out of school, out of work, and unable to obtain employment, is likely to become worse rather than better during the remaining years of the 1960's unless prompt and decisive action is taken to reverse this trend.

The foregoing conclusion is based on factors such as the following: (1) There will be an increasing number of youths aged 17 to 20 inclusive in the years just ahead; (2) the standards for admission to the military services are apparently being raised since some 50 per cent of those examined are rejected; (3) automation is decreasing the demand for unskilled labor, especially for youths without work experience and still subject to military call; and (4) discrimination against several minority groups of which Negroes are the largest.

There has been some gain in school retention as measured by the percentage of fifth-graders who continue through high school. In 1950, 504 of 1,000 fifth-graders finished high school. By 1962, this figure rose to 640.

This progress, however, needs to be considered in relation to the growing number of children who are reaching the high-school and post-high-school ages in the 1960's. They will enter a labor market plagued by chronic unemployment and unable to offer the opportunity to work, even to some high school graduates—particularly those lacking marketable skills.

An unprecedented growth in the labor force is in prospect for the United States during the 1960's as a result of the population explosion of the 1940's and later. In addition, if we assume no more than a continuation of the post-war increased rate in productivity, employment opportunities equivalent to over two million new jobs per year will be needed to offset advances in technology.

The foregoing facts and considerations suggest that prompt and effective action should be taken so that all youths up to age 22 be in school, employed, or combine the two. The public should be actively and constructively concerned with what happens to all youth until they have successfully made the transition from school to satisfactory employment.

Secretary of Labor, Willard Wirtz, recently took such a position when he said:

I suggest that automation demands that the educational system, in one form or another, assume the responsibility of seeing to it that nobody leaves school until he or she is prepared to do the kind of work which is available.

This position does not imply that all youths need to be in school in the ordinary sense of the term up to age 22. Nor does it propose that everyone be provided full employment or that such employment as is provided fall within the bailiwick of the schools.

Rather, it holds that society take action so that all youths up to age 22 have a seven- or eight-hour day occupied by the particular kind of education or training they should have—employment either by private industry or agencies similar to those already projected under public auspices, or by a combination of education, training, and employment.

Such a program would be of great importance in aiding many disadvantaged youths, namely, Negroes, Puerto Ricans, Mexican-Americans, American Indians, residents of Appalachia, and children of families such as migratory laborers.

We should not fool ourselves into thinking that white Americans do not need to be taken into account in a total commitment for an effective transition from school to satisfactory employment. One projection, based on conditions in 1963, estimates that in 1965 a total of 750,000 male youths will be out of school and out of work and that 593,000 of these will be white and 159,000 will be Negro. The percentage out of school and unemployed is higher among Negroes, but the number of whites involved is much larger due to the population ratio of 8 to 1 between white and non-white citizens.

Nor should we be concerned solely or

largely with youths who drop out of school at age 16 or 17. Studies indicate that by the time they reach age 19 or 20, the large majority of youths have found employment. However, some have become delinquents or are en route to becoming unemployable. It is imperative that we focus the full power of positive and preventive education on the latter group.

But we must also reevaluate what we are to do for those who continue in school well beyond the age of 16 or 17. It has been proposed in this paper that society's action for the effective education of youth be the continuance of education to age 22. This proposal is based on facts. As indicated in the figures given below, there is a steady rise in the percentage of male youth out of school and out of work between the ages of 14 to 20. The

Per cent of Males Out of School and Unemployed by Ages, 1960

	14	15	16	17	18	19	20	21 & 22
All Males	3.6	5.0	7.8	10.2	11.9	12.4	12.2	11.3
Whites	3.3	4.5	7.2	9.3	10.7	11.1	10.8	10.1
Non-White	5.9	7.7	11.8	16.5	20.8	22.1	22.9	21.0

first drop in this trend occurs at age 20, but the percentage still at loose ends at ages 21 and 22 remains high.

There is need, therefore, for rapid development of junior or community colleges. A few states, especially California and to a lesser extent, New York, have taken definitive action along these lines. These institutions should serve two functions. One, they should offer the first two years of college designed to be followed by transfer to a four-year college for completion of the baccalaureate. Two, they should provide a wide and carefully planned vocational and technical program of terminal courses for those about to enter the labor force. Every effort should be made to see that the academicians do not turn junior and community colleges into institutions which base selectivity on academic aptitude at a level above secondary schools.

Finally, there is the question of the college group, generally age 18 to 21 inclusive. The scope of public education should take full account of their situation. There is a woeful waste of human talent at this level. Studies have repeatedly shown that a considerable percentage of youth qualified to do college work never obtain the baccalaureate. A number of factors are involved. Money is one. The cost of college education in public as well as private institutions of higher education is rising. This is recognized by a variety of interests such as banks which are ready to make loans, insurance companies anxious to start college funds for children at birth, and federal and college officers who sound the praises of loans available under the National Defense Education Act. We also hear much about the availability of scholarships.

All this adds up to the fact that college education in the United States is not free. The family of average or below-average income, especially if it includes two or more children, finds it extremely difficult to finance a college education. In some cases such families are either totally unable or are able to manage only by extreme sacrifice which often results in mortgaging the future of the family or of other children. Furthermore, it appears that the trend is in the direction of making it more difficult for all—except some of the very brilliant who win scholarships and the financially fortunate—to pay for first-rate education at the post-high-school level. It appears that federal legislation which ostensibly seeks to ease this situation is designed so as to favor high-tuition institutions. It is not my purpose to argue the relative merits of higher education under private or public auspices. Rather, my purpose is to point out what I believe to be both an undemocratic and dangerous trend in higher education in the United States— the tendency to put an increasing share of the burden of costs for higher education on the family and individual and a decreasing share on the general public. The conditions under which a college student can obtain scholarship funds are often difficult and sometimes demeaning.

Recently I heard an extended explanation of how a prospective college student could obtain financial aid under the NDEA. The two governing principles were stated in two words—"need" and "worth." Need is determined by a family-means test. By filling out the necessary number of blanks and taking certain other measures to prove the poverty or near-poverty level of his family, a capable student can obtain some NDEA funds. Certification of worth is established by a series of searching questions which must be answered by the student. If he is found worthy of a college education, he can obtain some help to that end. The question arises as to whether our society demands that many who may not fully meet all criteria of "worthiness" at age 17 should have the opportunity to prove their worth in a college which is more interested in keeping them in school than in eliminating them.

In short, higher education seems to be reverting to the theory which first governed elementary and secondary education in the United States—that in order to be eligible a person must be either financially affluent or a proven indigent. This trend is wrong. The stage of development of education and the critical nature of the services which it must render to a technological economy in a dangerous world demand that higher education be a matter of general and imperative public concern. Its availability should not be determined largely by family condition and economics. It should be effectively free to all those able and willing to fulfill its demands.

How Shall We Define and Improve Quality in Education?

SOME WOULD DEFINE quality in education as selection and full development of the gifted. They would employ curricula, logically developed from the elementary and secondary school grades to the collegiate and postgraduate levels, which would lead to research in new fields of knowledge. This effort for excellence is one form of quality in education. It is important and must not be neglected, for it leads to new frontiers of knowledge. It equips many academically gifted youths for leadership in their chosen

72

fields. However, current concern with the highly talented, in my judgment, is too often leading to undue emphasis on grades, examinations, and standardized tests. Experience shows that creative minds frequently function in a manner which cannot be measured objectively. And, in some cases, geniuses are discouraged from developing their potential if there is insistence on set performances. Even curricula for the gifted must be designed to fit individual needs.

But quality in education in a democracy cannot be solely or even principally concerned with the gifted. Nor should quality in education be defined as the early elimination from school of all those not responsive to intellectual stimulation by a liberal arts or scientific curriculum. The commonplace mind of the average person, neither brilliant nor backward, is in my judgment, being neglected in favor of the gifted and the dull. This is particularly unfortunate, since those of average mental ability constitute the great bulk of our population.

In a democracy, quality in education seeks

to give each child and each youth the kind of education which will best enable him to discharge effectively his private and public duties. Quality education begins with the individual and ends by taking account of *all* individuals. A former superintendent of schools in a large, industrial city recently gave this definition of quality education:

Quality education is something which is applied to the individual at his level of culture and within his capabilities. You begin with the youngster where he is. Actually, in some cases, bathing takes precedence over reading, but reading should come along without delay.

Quality education must not only be relevant to the lives, experience, needs, and purposes of pupils; it must also be relevant to the age in which we live and to the great ideals which have shaped and moved our nation.

This means that the scope and purposes of education must not emphasize any single factor, be it intellectual development or vocational training. We must develop an educational program which ministers to the

74

well-being of all rather than a select few who are chosen on the basis of academic promise or social status. A developing program must envisage a wide range of aptitude and opportunity. It must take full account of the rising significance of education to the individual and to the social progress of the nation. This calls for educational opportunity so broad that it cannot be confined to any one area of knowledge or human concern. The emphasis will vary according to individual differences.

The drive for intellectual development as the sole purpose of education has its limitations, particularly when it takes the intolerant form of rejecting as uneducable those who, from choice or aptitude, do not respond to abstractions and revel in the contents of so-called "great books." The majority respond more effectively to concrete content which can be related to the many aspects of life. Also, there are great books based upon conceptions and experience indigenous to the free societies which have evolved in western Europe and the United States since the Renaissance. The worship of the so-called classics, which are the product of the slavocracy of Greece and Rome, can be overdone, especially when such content is rated as suitable and compulsory for all students. To summarize, quality in education necessitates that the talent of each child be sought out and developed to the fullest.

Quality in education cannot be improved without certain tangible and material resources. A modern school system to provide quality education must have an adequate staff of persons of differing and specialized competency and professional preparation. In addition to classroom teachers, school principals, and superintendents, school systems require librarians, school-attendance officers, playground supervisors, athletic directors, psychologists, guidance counselors, social workers, school nurses, and specialists who work with exceptional children. Included in this category are the gifted, those with language difficulties, the slow learners, the emotionally disturbed and mentally retarded, the hard-of-hearing, the physically handicapped, the homebound, the delinquent, and the pre-delinquent.

As to the desirable pupil-staff ratio in a public school system, there is considerable disagreement. A few wealthy school districts have as many as 70 professionals per 1,000 pupils. The national average is 40. The Educational Policies Commission has called for 50 professionals for 1,000 pupils. This is a realistic minimum. In the depressed areas of great cities it should be far higher—60 professionals per 1,000 pupils is a more reasonable figure.

Some argue that the pupil-teacher ratio could be reduced by adoption of various arrangements for instruction, such as: team teaching, programmed courses and teaching machines, teaching by television and similar application of mechanical instruction. How far such methods can reduce the pupil-teacher ratio and school costs, without losses in such vital matters as individual contact between pupil and teacher, has yet to be determined. Also, the cost factor involved in course-programming, the purchase of teaching machines and other mechanical devices, and their proper use and servicing, has yet to be adequately assessed.

The pupil-staff ratio will doubtless differ substantially in accord with such factors as the subject of instruction, the grade level and the type of pupils being instructed, the extent to which technical and vocational instruction is provided in either the upper years of high school or at the junior college level, and the amount of follow-up, guidance, education, and training provided those who now become "dropouts" at age 16 or 17.

To summarize, the first essential in improving quality of education is an adequate staff of persons differing in specialized competency and professional preparation. The personnel problem lies at the heart of achieving the kind of public school we want.

In recruiting and retaining a qualified staff favorable working conditions and adequate professional salaries are highly influential factors.

An effective learning environment should include the following favorable working conditions: (1) a continuing and well-conceived program which encourages and offers recognition to good teaching; (2) substantial freedom granted to the individual teacher's lesson content and method of achieving approved educational goals; and (3) community respect for education and appreciation of the teacher's calling. Research has shown that there is substantial correlation in a community between quality of schools and citizen perception of the components of good education. Such perception is the product of interest in and action for good schools by citizen and professional leadership.

Improvement in quality of education also requires that professional personnel in public schools be paid salaries equivalent to those in other professions which require equivalent training and responsibility.

Equipment, supplies, and textbooks for effective instruction, readily available in sufficient quantity, are essential to the improvement of quality in education. They are frequently inadequate. In efforts to raise teachers' salaries, some school boards have "economized" on some of the foregoing items, thus creating ill-effects on facilities available to teachers and services provided to pupils.

Expenditures for sites of school buildings as well as other long-term investments are essential to an improved quality in education. These expenditures will increase with the growth of school population and the diminishing availability of open space suitable for school grounds—a result of increasing population density.

Paying teachers competitive professional salaries, decreasing pupil-staff ratios, providing adequate equipment, supplies, and textbooks for effective instruction, and increasing capital outlays for sites and school buildings —these are all essential to improved quality in education. They all cost money. This raises the recurring question: Can the cost be met?

Can We Meet the Cost of Providing First-Rate Educational Opportunity for All?

THIS PAPER PROPOSES an extension in the scope of educational opportunity. Public education would begin at the nursery school level for some and at the kindergarten level for all. Education, training, and guidance would be made available to everyone until such time as a successful transition from school to work were effected. College education would be free for an increasing percentage of students. The curriculum of the American system of education would be differentiated to take account of the wide range in backgrounds, aptitudes, interests, and life goals of a heterogeneous population. The aim would be to develop each individual's talents to the full, whether he be a genius, a person of average aptitude, a slow learner, or one suffering mental or physical handicaps. Facilities for life-long adult learning and retraining which rapid change in occupational and other spheres of living now demand would be made more effective and more readily available than they are today.

A system of education of such scope and quality for a rising population will cost much more than is presently being expended. Various estimates have been made as to how much more would need to be spent. Let us say that it will cost at least twice what it is costing now. Some such increase should come in a matter of years rather than decades. Lest such an increase in educational expenditure be labeled chimerical, let us recall that total expenditures for public elementary and secondary schools in 1953-54 were barely $9 billion. Ten years later in 1963-64 these expenditures were over $21 billion—an increase of nearly two and a half times.

Can an additional increase for education

of this dimension be met? The answer to this question will be determined by several factors.

First and above all else is the priority which Americans place upon education. If lack of insight on the part of the people and ill-informed and outrageous attacks made upon public education and the educational establishment continue, the funds may not be forthcoming. But if the people understand that our unique and free system of public schools is one of the basic foundations upon which our open and affluent society has been built, and upon which a greater society must be built, they will take decisive and informed action to vote the requisite funds.

Our unparalleled productivity makes it possible to have everything we value highly. The current annual gross national product of $627 billion and personal income of $497 billion not only permits the standard necessities of food, shelter, and clothing, but also allows us luxuries and even extravagant and ostentatious expenditures on a scale never before possible. To say that such an economy cannot afford the current $20 to $25 billion, or whatever additional amount is required to put public education on an adequate financial base, is sheer nonsense. Nevertheless, choices must be made. Mere exhortation on the importance of education is not enough. We must not succumb to shrill demands that there be no more taxes for anything. We must appreciate the value of education enough to take informed and decisive action in order to provide the funds necessary to finance first-rate public schools in every locality in the nation.

Merely to understand that our economy can afford excellent schools for all is not enough. This view of education focuses only on the consumption side of the economic ledger. Education, to be sure, is a high order of consumption. Education for intellectual development, for perceptive minds, and for intelligent discrimination in public and private affairs is demanded more today than ever before. The danger is, however, that when educational expenditure is thought of solely in these lofty terms, it is likely to be fiscally starved. This fosters the viewpoint

84

that school expenditure is something on which we must "save" if investment, economic growth, and jobs are to be forthcoming. The assumption is that investment in private industry is the sole base of economic progress. The free enterprise order is often extolled to the point that it is pictured as the "open sesame" to freedom and human well-being. Milton Freedman, Professor of Economics at the University of Chicago, illustrates this emphasis in the following quotation:

Wherever men are today reasonably free and relatively prosperous, they have gained their freedom and earned their prosperity through a system based on private property, free enterprise, and free markets. There is not a single exception.

I take no issue with this statement. But I would add that a private enterprise order alone guarantees nothing. For every nation operating under the free play of so-called classical economic law which is relatively prosperous, there is another so operating which wallows in dire poverty.

Let us add to Professor Freedman's statement the following facts. Nowhere in the world today can one find a nation "reasonably free and relatively prosperous," which lacks an effective system of education. As pointed out in the first section of this paper, one can fairly well estimate the degree of prosperity of a nation by knowing the percentage of its population which is literate. It is not natural resources which determine the prosperity of a nation. Studies have shown that some nations with the most meager natural resources stand high in per capita production, and that some which possess fabulous natural resources are near the bottom in economic status.

The conditions described above and information gleaned in a recent search of economists for the source of economic growth reveal that investment in education is an essential accompaniment if not a precursor of such growth. The latter appears to be the case in at least some nations.

This is not to deprecate the importance of a free economy and investment in private industry. Rather, it is to point out the importance of investment in education. Economists are saying that educational investment which would build intelligent citizens and a highly trained labor force ranks in economic importance with investment in factories, power plants, and other industrial establishments.

This highly significant fact is also coming to be recognized by thoughtful business executives. Business firms are investing substantial sums to retrain and further educate their personnel. This expenditure, however, must usually be based upon high levels of education and training prior to entering the labor force. Recent efforts at training the unemployed have encountered some sobering facts. Many of the unemployed are unemployable because they are untrainable. And they are untrainable because they lack the basic education to take the kind of training required to fill jobs for which there is a demand. The correlation between learning and earning is too well known to require elaboration.

We are on the verge of an era when education will no longer be looked upon as a semi-luxury to be enjoyed only by the few.

The argument that a society "saves," regardless of effects, by cutting school budgets to the bone, to use a favorite phrase of the "down with taxes" crowd, will be recognized as a myth. On the positive side, we will look upon a proper balance between investment in things and in people as the sine qua non of a free and viable society.

As this policy is put into action many distressing social ills, which have their roots in educational neglect and denial of educational opportunity, will be attacked at their source. No longer will a considerable percentage of youth drop out of school at ages 14, 15, 16 and 17. We will view this practice as part of a primitive stage in our educational evolution. The community and the school will know that the social cost of tossing thousands of uneducated and untrained youths into the type of labor market which technology has brought about is what we cannot afford. We will see that the racial problem in the United States has its roots in inequality and even denial of educational opportunity for Negro children and youth. The full power of educa-

88

tion will be brought to bear on the people of Appalachia and other pockets of poverty and educational neglect. No youth with ability and incentive, merely because his family is poor, will find it impossible to enter and complete college. We will look back upon our hesitant efforts to make higher education effectively free as we now view the time when it was expected that only a fraction of our citizens would learn to read and write.

We hold that well-conceived and adequately financed educational programs are requisite in achieving and maintaining a viable society. Neglect of education is paid for in social and economic ills such as unemployment, unemployability, relief, and other nonproductive conditions.

What are the means which will be used to raise the substantial sums required to capitalize the full power of education in the Great Society? In short, just how are we going to raise the revenue required?

First, some money will come from local taxation. We will continue to recognize that local tax effort is basic to local interest and initiative in public education.

The principal source of local revenue will continue to be the property tax. It will be supplemented by local non-property taxes, and especially so in large counties and in our populous city-states. Areas made up of a number of local school districts may be consolidated for taxation purposes. This would tend to even out inequalities in taxability and would improve the effectiveness of administration of both the property tax and of local non-property taxes.

Two changes would strengthen the keystone of local school support—the property tax. First, the proportion of support coming from this tax should be generally decreased and especially so in school districts with little tax capacity. We should study the financing of education in our congested cities. The educational problems which migration has brought to urban areas have originated largely outside their boundaries and cannot be solved solely with locally-raised revenue. This is due partly to the heavy cost of remedial education, and is further complicated by the high cost of many other forms of public action required for urban renewal.

A second major reform of the property tax has to do with its structure and administration. Taxation of property should increasingly be on tangible as opposed to intangible property. Assessments should be made equitable either by improving the efficiency and honesty of local assessors or by state action in correcting inequitable assessment. This is especially important in allocating state funds in which local tax capacity is one factor in the formula.

State limitation on local property tax rates for education should be abolished, especially in school districts where boards of education are elected by the people. At the least, local tax assessors should not be permitted to dilute local tax limits imposed by the state by chronic under-assessment of property.

The second source of adequate funds for public education will be the state level of government. Property as the principal source of revenue for public schools is an anachronism in a nation in which trade and industry have replaced agriculture as the major source of income. This fact lies back of the virtual abolition of state property taxation. At the same time, new state taxes, in tune with changes in economic conditions, are being adopted. The principal sources of state revenue now are taxes on sales and income, licenses, and other miscellany.

However, these categories are found in balanced proportion in only a few states. A considerable percentage of states do not levy personal or corporate income taxes. Others do not have sales taxes, or at most they are not imposed on sales in general, but on only a few commodities such as gasoline, liquor, or tobacco.

Many state tax structures are a hodgepodge. While they raise some revenue to finance state undertakings and aid localities in financing education and local undertakings, state tax structures, often the product of special interest pressures, are not as broadly-based as might be desired. In some states a great game is played with two competing teams. One group resolutely stands for no new taxes, regardless of the need for adequate support of schools and other public undertakings. The goal of the game is to see that the other group bear new taxes, if, because of public needs generated by a complex, interdependent and technological society, the position of the first group cannot be maintained. Hence, one group will insist on enactment of an income tax but no sales tax, while another group insists on a sales but no income tax.

The states differ radically in percentage of public school revenue coming from the state. In 1962-63 this ranged between 70 and 80 per cent in Delaware, New Mexico, and North Carolina and between 6 and a little over 10 per cent in Nebraska, New Hampshire and South Dakota. For the nation as a whole, the per cent of state revenue allocated to public elementary and secondary schools in 1962-63 was 39.3 per cent. In Pennsylvania it was 42.1 per cent.

However, it has become increasingly clear that even a fairly broad system of state taxation, along with local taxes, will not provide adequate tax revenue for public undertakings, including public schools. Between the turn of the century and about 1956 the percentage of public school revenue coming from the state more than doubled. It apparently reached a plateau of about 40 per cent in 1956 and has remained there since. This percentage along with local support and the federal government's pittance of about 4 per cent is not enough to finance the type of educational programs our society demands.

Accordingly, the third and most powerful level of government has come into the picture. The issue of federal aid for education is only part of the total landscape. Nearly all categories of public enterprise are receiving or are about to receive federal support. The forces which are bringing this about are numerous. Only a few can be identified in this paper.

The first factor is that the demand for public services has outrun the resources which the states and localities can in actual fact command. This is true not only of the so-called poor states, but it also applies to rich states such as New York and California. The states cannot do the job alone because in actual performance they lack power to raise tax revenue comparable to that of the federal government.

One often hears it said that income upon which all taxes rest is not increased by transferring the collection of taxes from the state to the federal level. This is true, but it is irrelevant. The practical fact is that taxable capacity shows great genius in dodging or avoiding its proper share of the tax load when it deals with individual localities and states. This powerful influence against tax reform is absent when the federal government is concerned. Some states and localities go to the most extreme lengths to attract business enterprises into their territory by giving them tax preferment or even tax exemption. Business enterprises already within a state oppose needed tax reform by claiming that it will put them at an economic disadvantage in competing with industry in other states. These are specious arguments, but to a substantial degree, they defeat state efforts to

provide adequate financing of public education.

Another factor which has made the federal government the collector of two-thirds
of all tax revenue is the recognition that we
are a nation and an interdependent one at
that. To have attempted to finance our heavy
expenditures for military defense by using
state funds to expand the militia of the several states would have been ridiculous. The
same applies to unemployment, relief, and
social security. Our highway construction
would have been even slower if only state
funds and state agreements had advanced
this area of public concern.

The one area of mounting national interest,
largely neglected by the federal government,
is public education. The forces in back of this
failure are too well known to need specifica-
tion. The fact is that the federal government
has doubly short-changed education. It has
appropriated a mere pittance of revenue toward public elementary and secondary school
support. At the same time it has been relatively generous in financing other areas of

broad national concern. There are those who would condemn this practice, but the recent election does not promise a reversal in the use of federal funds to finance public undertakings of national concern.

This being the case, any area of public enterprise which receives little or no federal aid is at a severe disadvantage. The disadvantage is increased when the state must make some contribution to the public undertaking involved. When a state can receive a dollar from the federal government for each dollar it contributes in financing an undertaking, this state raises its share as experience has demonstrated. An undertaking is even more favored when, as in the case of some highway construction, the state receives 90 cents by contributing 10 cents. Public education receives very little federal support under such attractive conditions. This is a major reason why public schools encounter hard going in many state legislatures.

The tragic fact is that in spite of obvious need, Congress has failed to vote grants for public elementary and secondary education comparable to those granted to nearly every other area of national concern. This has happened in spite of recommendations made by every United States President from Roosevelt to Johnson. This inaction by Congress is one of the past generation's greatest failures in statesmanship.

It is encouraging, however, that the issue of federal aid for public education will not go away in spite of the efforts of some to this end. As a recent Congressional study on this matter states, federal aid is no longer an issue; it is a fact.

The federal government must be further and substantially involved in the financing of education for several reasons. First, it is logical. Education is more than a matter of local and state concern. No unscalable walls separate our states. Migration transfers the results of educational neglect to our congested cities, and in the process, multiplies the social ills spawned by such neglect. As Walter Lippmann recently said: "The cause of the poverty which still remains is not the maldistribution of wealth but a shortage of education."

98

President Hannah of Michigan State University, after seven years as Chairman of the United States Commission on Civil Rights, concludes that the real solution of the civil rights problem "won't come until we raise a whole generation of Negroes who have had a good education from kindergarten through college."

Nor should we look upon the abolition of poverty and assumption of the rights and duties of educated citizens as affecting only Negro citizens. The total number of white persons who suffer from poverty and educational denial exceeds the number of Negroes so deprived.

There are encouraging signs on the horizon. The 88th Congress enacted some significant educational legislation. Better financed schools was one of the items advocated by President Johnson in the 1964 campaign, and his recent policy paper on education is a first-rate statement.

However, those who believe in educational opportunity for all should not content themselves with federal legislation which has been enacted to date. They must see that it be put into effective operation. But this is still only a beginning step. What further needs to be done?

We should recognize that the so-called selective approach to federal financing of education is merely a new name for an old practice—special rather than general aid to provide a sound educational foundation for every child in the land.

Recent federal legislation will provide only a small fraction of the total cost of an effective nation-wide system of education. True even at the level of higher education where much of the new federal money is concentrated, it is more evident yet at the public elementary and secondary school level. Recent federal legislation is strong on ideas for improving education, but weak in providing substantial funds to finance such improvement.

Selective federal education legislation implements what Congress thinks is important. It finances initiative from the federal level

100

rather than that of state and local Boards of Education. This is federal control.

One of the ironies of the past generation has been the repeated exhortations in Congress, and indeed nearly everywhere, against the dangers of federal control of education, while at the same time one measure after another inherently involving federal control has been enacted.

What are some of the guides to future action in developing a sound program of federal financial support of education?

First, every effort should be made to make the special aids or categorical grants now in effect, and those enacted in the future, as effective as possible. Those which get results should be extended, and those which do not should be discontinued. This is easier said than done. More immediate is the problem of effective administration of recently enacted special grants. Some of these entail the setting up of new administrative machinery which involve the federal government and one or both of state and local levels of government. The battles, political and otherwise, which will be waged to control these new education-oriented measures will be vigorous. This factor plus the inherent difficulties encountered in developing essentially new types of educational services could lead to a discrediting of all federal intervention in education.

Second, there should be no lessening in the drive to secure general federal aid for public education. This is essential if the scope and quality of public education, as outlined earlier in this paper, are to be achieved. Such a system of education far transcends local and private concern—important as they are. Without first-rate education for all in every part of the nation, our unity, common purpose, and quest for equal opportunity will be severely threatened.

The Acts which allocate funds to federally-affected school districts are the closest that we have come to achieving substantial general federal support for public schools. I refer to school districts where military or defense undertakings have caused an influx of school children, and in some cases, a decrease in taxable property. These Acts should not be viewed simply as temporary measures; they should be strongly supported and extended to other school districts. What local school district is not federally-affected, if by no other fact than that the federal government collects two-thirds of all public revenue?

The suggestion has been made to allocate to the states a fixed proportion of each year's federal income tax collections. Under present conditions affecting the need for additional school revenue, the states might be expected to allocate a substantial part of this to public school support. Although this would be indirect general support of schools, it could contribute substantially to their financing.

Third, there is the danger that recent legislation may further distort distribution of support as it affects certain levels and types of education. Two illustrations of this are described below.

One is the bias in favor of higher education, public and private, and in the disfavor of public elementary and secondary education. I believe that if in regard to this, one had to make a choice, elementary and secondary education should be assigned priority for financial aid.

Furthermore, in at least some respects it appears that the wealthier institutions of higher education—both public and private, especially the latter—are favored over those that most need federal aid. One Congressional study has pointed out that a highly disproportionate amount of federal research money is being granted to a few of the most heavily endowed colleges and universities. The effects of a practice such as this are far-reaching and too numerous to permit detailed exploration in this paper. Suffice it to say that influential opinion concerning the financing of education in general and higher education in particular is based often on limited viewpoints of the role of education as an agency of national viability. A recent speech by a top official of one of our largest corporations raises a number of fundamental issues about the financing of education in general and about the trend of some of the recent federal legislation which affects education. His statement follows:

I think economic growth is impaired when a state absorbs so much of the cost of public higher education facilities that our invaluable network of private colleges and universities is financially jeopardized. I feel very strongly about this problem; I speak as a trustee of a private college and an educational foundation. State colleges and universities have an important role to play in our society, but I wonder whether they should charge so relatively little tuition and other fees that competing private colleges and universities increasingly cannot charge enough to enable them to pay the salaries required to hold good faculty and administrative people.

Should we not expect the main beneficiaries of public undergraduate and graduate education —namely, the students and their parents—to pay a more realistic share of the cost? If they don't, the cost must be borne by taxpayers generally.[7]

Our aim should be the development of an educational structure—strong, coordinated, and well-financed at all levels—rather than

[7] Robert C. Tyson (Chairman, Finance Committee, U.S. Steel Corporation), *Private Impact of Public Spending* (New York: Public Relations Department, U.S. Steel, 1964).

105

the improvement of a few private institutions whose student bodies are, for the most part, economically and socially secure. This is imperative if we are to meet the rising educational demands of our dynamic and complex society. National security and progress are too dependent on the scope and quality of multilevel education to allow financing to be determined merely in terms of individual benefits or financial resources.

A broad orientation concerning education is not represented by much recent federal educational legislation. Substantial funds are provided for top educational levels, but relatively little is provided to carry the greater part of educational costs at the base of the educational pyramid. We lose too much talent in the first ten or twelve years of schooling. Too many with adequate aptitude never get far enough to receive the benefits of a college or junior or community college education. This fact is not sufficiently recognized in the federal education legislation which has been enacted to date.

Recent federal education legislation threat-

ens a second distortion in educational expenditure. Much of this legislation emphasizes
curative rather than preventive measures. It
is requisite that attempts be maximized to
cure the ills of educational neglect as they
become evident in the form of unemployment
resulting from a lack of functional literacy in
youths between 14 and 17. Educational action
to aid adult illiterates is also essential. Recent
federal legislation, however, is too much
limited to correcting educational deficiencies
which sometimes are beyond the stage of
correction. It is not enough to be concerned
with the prevention of educational deficiencies. It is highly important that the full power
of education be used to prevent educational
ills which originate in young children and
multiply later under substandard educational
conditions.

Education is of such fundamental concern
to individual and general well-being and
viability that its support cannot be left solely
to the varied financial resources of the individual state, locality, and individual citizen.
Federal leadership based on modern concep-

tions of the indispensability of education in maintaining cultural, social, and economic growth is also essential. Education at all levels must be effectively free for all. Failure in this regard not only denies the individual's right, but also threatens the foundations of a free and viable society.

Horace Mann in one of his final addresses to the graduating class of Antioch College in 1859 beseeched his audience to "be ashamed to die until you have won some victory for humanity." There are yet many victories to be won.